A Journey
Through Love

A Journey Through Love

Poetry by Shaquan Lewis

Writing Journey 101 Press

A Journey Through Love
© 2023 Shaquan Lewis
ISBN: 978-1-961523-01-2

First Edition, 2023

Printed in the United States of America

Cover Photo by Javaun Bruins
Cover Design by Emily Anne Evans
Interior Layout Design by Adrianna D. Ford

Contents

Preface

Love is of the essence
If this love I desire only exists within my dreams
Please don't wake me up

On this day the world can
Metaphorically of course yet still literally
hold my heart in its hand
Rip out pages and cry with me
Tears of joy from me no longer
Reminiscing on the heartbreaks
That made this heart beat broken
With each page turned I wipe away the troubles tribulations the trauma
and I make love in its rawest form beautifully again
This book be thy blessing to heal in my hands the healing strong
It doesn't apologize for being the truth
It is and forever will be
How I leave my legacy
Heart on my sleeve or in other words
In this book I bleed

Acknowledgements

I would first like to thank God for everything that he has done for me and everything he is going to do, thank you for this gift to write, thank you for the love in my heart may my broken heart help heal someone else's.

I would like to thank my parents Monique and Robert for doing the very best of their ability to give and show me love in the only way they knew how. I would like to thank my Nanny and my Auntie Lynn for being there when I needed them. Pa Pa you were the first reason why I started to write poetry. I thank God for my friends and family—both blood and through the mud—Johnny my love, Danny, Raven, Tae, Shay, the Go to Work Lady

I thank my poetry family from Da Poetry Lounge, Spoken Lit, CLI, Street Poets. I want to thank my poetry teachers Poetri Smith, Alyesha Wise, Matthew Cuban, Edwin Bodney, Ravina, Tommy Domino, James Coats and Hiram Sims. Thank you to my tribe Verses and Vibes.

Andrea thank you for your sponsorship, your encouragement for letting your light shine. Ebony you are the greatest I can't thank you enough. D (Adrianna) you have been heaven sent, you are amazing. I want to thank my exes for some of these poems, My first Love Javaun, my current love Jay and all the loves in between for igniting all these feelings of love.

I love all my siblings Rob, Trev, Taylor, Dee, TaKia I am proud of all of you. I want to thank my sister Shyann for being my rock, my best friend, my reason for being. You are everything to me and I don't know what I would do without you. I love you more than anything in this world, nobody can take your place as my rider, my partner in crime, my right hand, the first person I call in any situation. My heartbeat is my sister Shy.

Forgive me those who I have failed to mention, thank you for all the love.

Last but not least, I want to thank me for believing in me, for not giving up on me, and for trusting me in the process.

A Journey
Through Love

My heart is

damaged

BUT

sometimes you gotta go through the pain
to know the experience, the joy ...
you go through some choas
to acknowledge peace
cry it out to embrace that smile

A Look at Love

Pain can be so beautiful
depending on how you look at it
only you can determine how you look at life
you can take the good with the bad
The bad and the good and make a miracle
do you believe in miracles
that anything is possible
when you wish upon a star do you believe it will
come true

I do

I believe anything is possible
if you believe
Do you believe in love
that love is a miracle
no matter how many times love lets you down
do you find yourself loving again

I do

After all the heartbreaks broken promises and
relationships that have ended on a bad note
I still have hope
I still believe in love
That real love
That unconditional love
That kind of love
That love you don't have to question
Love without a doubt
Love is somewhere out there waiting for me
Somewhere just beyond the horizon
so close that I could almost see it

I Love You

I told myself to stop expecting so much from love
Expectations lead to disappointments
But how can I be disappointed in you?

I love you

Remembering:
To be patient
Be kind
Hold no record of wrong
          I try not to acknowledge the pain and poke at open wounds
            I'll ignore the fact that you kissed someone else
             Fucked a girl in the bed where we laid
           It's not like it was your intention to hurt me
               You were just being a man

               Shit happens

        You couldn't have possibly known I wanted you all to myself
            That I was willing to wait for your love
           We were supposed to run away you and I
               Travel the world

     You couldn't tell by looking in my eyes I was expecting you to
        read my mind about how much I loved you
          I should have told you my vision of us
           told you if we remained close
          We should get married

Should have told you to propose
I never wanted to let you go
Should have reminded you on how I thought
we were made for each other
we made each other better

          Your hard head
          My soft lips

               You were the only one I wanted to kiss
         You were the only one I could see me spending the rest of my
                   life with

       How come you couldn't see it
      I was expecting a romantic experience
     Instead I've got an interesting story to tell
       About a love I hate that I love
       And now I have to leave behind
         When I still love you

Flowers and Love

Roses are red…Violets are blue ish … I guess…
Actually violets are violet…It is what it is…. Love…
is complicated…love can love you one day and not
so much the next. Like flowers they die…It takes
time for it to grow again…It has its seasons….blooms
and transitions…Needs nourishment before the
plucking…Some cut it too short…Some are
long-stemmed…Others thorned for
protection…Love could be so
simple
…But like flowers
rooted from
a dark place
Looking towards the light
Withstanding
the rain
Even with
petals falling
still love
be a
part of its
name
Whatever kind
of flower it
may be
Love be thy
bouquet
carefully
picked
Held close walking
down the
aisle
but when it's
all said and
done
I don't want to
throw it away

Condescending Love

Your sorrow runs deep
You keep exuding light
Head held high overlooking the low blows
Tripping on the thought of being ... yet
Still
S
T
A
N
D
I
N
G
Firm
on Love

Smile

```
S                    S
M                    M
I                    I
L                    L
E        Always      E
```

Even when you're crying you smile * Your smile could save a life today * They need your smile

Keep Smiling

Come Love

Love comes to me
When it wants to feel safe

My energy says you are welcomed here
No judgment

Just a shoulder to lean on
An ear to listen

…But who's gonna be that for me…

Mary Jane?
            Hennessy?
                        My smile?

                    Love

Love Lessons

My mother taught me that there is a good and bad side to everyone.

My father taught me that the ones you love the most can disappoint you.

Love is schizophrenic

How It Is

It be like that sometimes
In a blink of an eye
All that you know to be true
All that you love
Changes
It just be like that
Be like that time we thought
we had a lover
Be like that time we thought
we had a friend
But that thing we thought we had
It ended up hurting us in the end
Hurt us worse than any enemy done ever did
And it be like that
Like they really bamboozled me
Straight fraud
Like we didn't have history
Like they really did that to me
Hurt me
But you see it be like that

Be like I'd never but do
Be like I wouldn't but will
Be like I can but won't
Not about to bother
To stoop down to
A level beneath me
Not about to wait
For someone to swoop me up out
The mess they left me in
I cried rivers into oceans with my love
They didn't even bother to say my bad or oh well
Eventually you'll get over it
Unfortunately, it be like that
Fortunately, I'll be that bitch
That phoenix that rises from the ashes
That walks despite the slaughter
'Cause it be like that
Be like grim
Be like reaper
Be that kill them with kindness
curse them with words of love
Even though they don't be like that
Be like this
Undefeated
Powerful
Be like God
Be like Gs like us
Poets turning pain into power

11

A Journey to Love

I'm on that journey to find the kind of love that I could only imagine

I say imagine 'cause I can't say I ever really had the kind of love
I'm looking for
I've had love but not the kind of love I desire

I'm definitely on a quest to find it

A journey to love
I'm on a journey
I want to be loved
I need to be loved

I'm talking about that real love

That LOVE love

That kind of love that makes you feel healed love
Not the kind of love that forgets you exist or blocks
you when they're PISSED

I'm talking 'bout that unconditional love

That pinky promise -
cross my heart and hope to die
If I ever forget how much I LOVE you type love

That make it look easy on a Sunday morning kind of
Love

And even though it gets hard sometimes we're still in love

I want that "Notebook" love
When we wake up to LIVE and die in each other's arms love
So in love

The kind of love they'll write stories about...

When it seems like a fairy tale but it's just how we love
The kind of love that'll have me sitting up all night
writing songs about how I will always love you

But I ain't going nowhere love

I will stay for love

Pray for love

I want that LOVE love

I want *kisses* on the forehead in the middle of the day
and before I go to sleep

I want sunflower showers
honeycomb hideout
Love like a sweet treat
Make my cheeks tingle

I want love notes for no reason
Calls just to say I'm thinking of you love

I want walks on the beach

An endless amount of anniversaries
celebrations of our love over everything

Smiling like everyday's my birthday from the way
that love loves me

I want that kind of love
you know
like that
Shihan Love Like This
type poem

That love love
I know it's a journey

…

I'm going through it to find it

Bleeding Love

I thought that time would have healed me by now
but I still cry

A healing is still in order
Feels like I'll never get over losing love

It withered after the years

Still feels <u>alive</u> to me
Not quite *dead* yet

I can still hear love's voice calling…

…Telling me you are mine

Wish it really was you
Wish it really was true
Wish it was really love

Wish I could tell love how I really feel

How I never want to let it go
That love be the very breath I

b r e a t h e

And I did and love still goes on

I imagine if all the tears I've ever cried from a
heartbreak were to fill this room

Love would watch me d
r
o
w
n

Wouldn't care to send a kiss a hug or any kind of love

And I still would fix my lips to say
"I love you"

'Cause I do
This hurt is love too

Love is still around though distant
Love has made it perfectly clear that:

Love don't love me today
Will not love me tomorrow
Will think about it for future reference

Got me questioning the love I thought I had

Like was it just a part of my imagination

Did I imagine love?

I never questioned it
I could have been hallucinating

As if I
never felt like I was doing too much
As if I
never felt like we should take it slow

That didn't happen

I'm still picking up the pieces of broken glass
From the crash
When love was mad

When love decided to shatter every picture
I ever thought of what love could have been it

~~Cut deep~~

I'm still

B
L
E
E
D
I
N
G

Obsessed

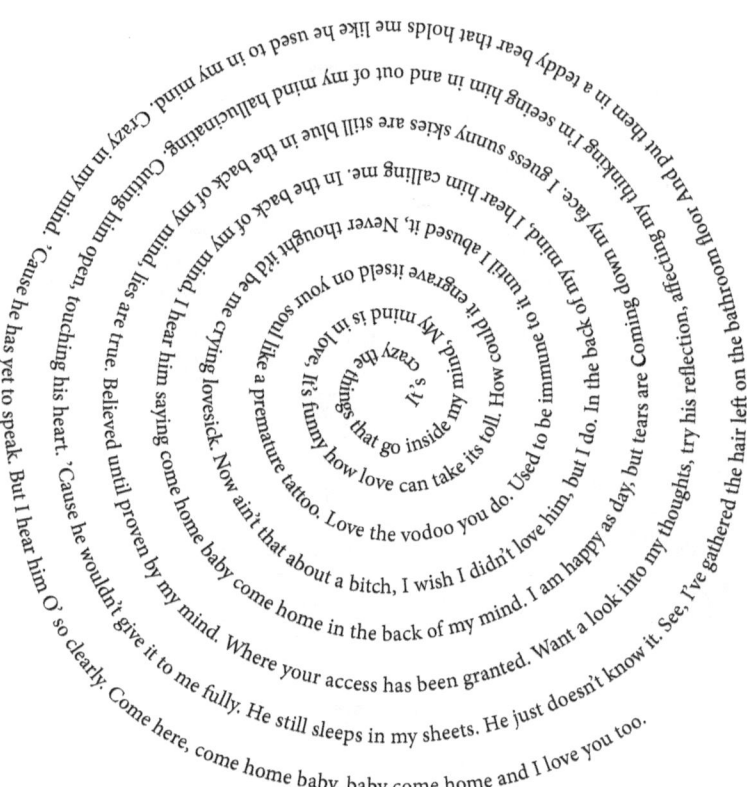

It's Crazy the things that go inside my mind. My mind is in love. It's funny how love can take its toll. How could it engrave itself on your soul like a premature tattoo. Love the vodoo you do. Used to be immune to it until I abused it, Never thought it'd be me crying lovesick. Now ain't that about a bitch, I wish I didn't love him, but I do. In the back of my mind. I do. In the back of my mind, I hear him calling me. In the back of my mind, I hear him saying come home baby come home in the back of my mind. Where your access has been granted. I am happy as day; but tears are Coming down my face. Want a look into my thoughts, try his reflection, affecting my thinking I'm seeing him in and out of my mind hallucinating. And put them in a teddy bear that holds me like he used to in my mind. Crazy in my mind. He still sleeps in my sheets. He just doesn't know it. See, I've gathered the hair left on the bathroom floor. Where your access has been granted. Now ain't that about a bitch, I wish I didn't love him, but I do. I guess sunny skies are still blue in the back of my mind, I hear him saying come home baby come home in the back of my mind. Cutting him open, lies are true. Believed until proven by my mind. He wouldn't give it to me fully. 'Cause he wouldn't give it to me fully. Cutting him open, touching his heart. 'Cause he has yet to speak. But I hear him O' so clearly. Come here, come home baby, baby come home and I love you too.

16

Mmtch

People say they love you
but do they really

What does it mean to really love somebody

Does it mean I deal with you untill you do something I don't like
Then I'm not going to deal with you until I feel like dealing with you again

Is love possesive?
Meaning,
if I don't do what you say
when you say
then you're not going to love me?

I thought love was
1 CORINTHIANS 13 VERSE 4
and so on

Where is the love of God in us
Why do we fall so short of the word to those we say we love
I'm guilty aparently love is suppose to keep secrets

The secret is fuck love

Don't play with my heart

I don't fight fair

I bust windows and slap *bitches*

Might bust a cap in yo ass if I have to

That's what love can do
Love can get it
Got me twisted

I can say fuck you and still love you

Love is a battlefield

...

are you ready for war?

Pa Pa's blood is splattered on the sidewalk...The teddy bear caught on fire from the burning candle....We are support to be praying...The family is not alking...The tension is so LOUD

Call It What You Want

He says that I don't love him
That I don't know what love is…

…I don't argue with that
I don't know

All I know is how I feel
And what these feelings make me do
I call it love
There's a possibility that there is another word that
can take its place
What do you call it when everything makes you
think of him

When the sun
The moon
The stars
All of the sky

Say his name

When every song played sounds like everything
we been through…

…Going through going to ...
Even silence screams their grace

In a blank space you can see their smile
Would walk
a thousand miles
Just to be close
even if not to touch
What do you call this

if not love

Obsession maybe…

…Call it crazy

What does it mean when
every time they walk away it
Gets harder to breathe
When the butterflies burst

When you see them calling
When your heart skips a beat
from the thought of
them

What is that

They say to get over someone you gotta get under
somebody else...

...What if that don't work?
What if not even good dick could fuck him out of my head

I tried to pray him away
At least I tried
I wrote songs about him
Every poem I write he is in
If this is not love
Tell me what it is

I would like to call it by its name
Infatuation?
Desperation?
A fatal attraction?

If it isn't love
Why do I feel this way?
Why can't I get him off my mind?
Is this just an addiction
I'm willing to overdose myself on?
'Cause I'll make exceptions and excuses to disregard all the bullshit he do

Just to love him to be loved by him...

...I'll come to some sort of understanding
It's dumb if it isn't love

Call it what you want
Love is what I call it

He says that not it
I have yet to come up with another explanation

I Know

I know
> what I know

I know
> I don't know it all

I know
> I want to understand what love is

I know
> what I want it to be

I know
> love is patient

I know
> love is kind

I know
> love is not necessarily like this all the time

I know
> love can hurt

Love
> could leave you stranded

Love
> could forget it ever even loved you

I know
I know
> love comes and goes

I know
> I want it stay

I know
> I don't know when it's real from when it's fake

I know
> I don't know if I've had it to say

I know
I know
> pieces of love

The breaks the hills the valleys
Love comes in many forms I know

It's not always going to go the way I want it

I don't know when love is right
And I don't know when love is wrong

Either way I keep holding on

I know
        love can make you do good
I know
        it can also make you go bad
Love
        can either lift you up
        Or have you fall on your ass

It's still love
        I'll take any way I can get
Love
        to be loved
I know
        it's the only reason I'm existing
Love
        don't live here no more

It just comes by to visit
capture love in a picture

that's one way to make it everlasting
The only way that I know

Don't talk about the blood bleed

What's left of the hole in my heart

Tengo un corazon para amar

I don't even know what that means

Broken Love

Do you hear the rain
Do you feel my pain
Do you feel the love
I don't
How does it feel
Can it heal

Heal all this pain that I feel
When my heart is aching
When my eyes are breaking
Breaking into tears
Tears that make my ocean
An ocean that doesn't move
No wave

'Cause nobody's there
to make the change
To my heart that is aching
To the tears that I am making
To people that are dying
To the family that
once was but no longer

'Cause they didn't feel the love

Head over hills in love

He takes her breath away

She felt as if she couldn't

B R E A T H E

without him

A Father's Love

My father who art in
heaven and on earth
My heaven on earth
My LIGHT when I'm
in a dark place I call
him

Dad...Friend...Best Friend...The definition of love...Oh, how I love my father...I
weep ....He soothes my oceans...Rides the waves with me to the shore...Oh, what a
hell of a ride it is. Our story not as complicated as it seems...A beautiful tragedy
An almighty delight of "Get your shit together"..My father hallowed be thy name

Robert be thy name
Bruce be thy name
James be thy name
LOVE
be they name
Oh Johnny, I come to
Thee with an open
heart. Hands up and
eyes closed 'cause I
trust you, see you, feel
you

I know you will never
let me...g o
I won't let you die
You can't die

You live through me
My savior my shoulder
to lean on
My amazing grace
How blessed I be that
I can say
That I know you

Not only do I know you,
but you are mine
My gift upon arrival
My love
My father
Amen

Church

When
they said come as
you
are...
I'm
assuming
they expected me
to make the change before
walking through the doors. What?
My mohawk shows defiance. Betta straighten
it out and lay it down like the rest of my burdens.
Before entering the house of the Lord.Clearly come as you
are means something totally different here. My skirt too short
to sing in the choir on Sunday morning.I guess I oughta take
my praise and worship back to shower or in my bed. Where I
am accepted fully naked. Baptized in the holy name. Or not.
Guess all this fabulousness makes it look like I got the devil
up in me. I ain't jumping for joy at all this judgement. I betta
clap my hands and wave them. They're watching. Bet they
think 'cause tears are falling from my eyes. That means my
joy has been taken. But joy is in me now, I'm not waiting till
the morning. Deemed me heathen 'cause I smell like a
Jamaican.They don't even bother to get to know my name
Just wanted my tides and offerings. Hoping I come back again
but I think I'll just pray at home. Or in my car like I usually do

Not just on Sunday

Her

She is pretty
Beautiful even

Not ashamed to get ugly with it
She's always wanting to present herself as free

She's salty but sweet
An off-balance of too nice

Nowhere close to mean enough

She knows the meaning of love

Knowing nothing about it

She's the girl with a big smile

Who cries a lot
A whole lot
Maybe too much

She has so many secrets

But she tells them all

An open and closed book
The pages unreadable
A bunch of scribble scrabble
Use your imagination

She will go wherever you tell her to go

But she's going to do whatever she wants to

She mainly focuses on convincing herself she's truly happy
She is truly happy
She is really happy some days

On some days she pretends

Pray Love

I pray
when I'm doing good I pray
when I'm doing bad I pray

I pray
And I promise God always makes a way

Becareful of what you pray for

I pray I don't go back to selling dope
And just be dope

A bitch be a trap Queen
A bitch will really get down in the trenches if need be

I pray for guidance
I pray for salvation

I pray I'm moving in the right direction
I pray that I make moves, boss moves

That God makes a way out of no way
I pray for better days

I pray I got something to live for
some thing to hold on to

I pray for the times ahead
I thank God in advance

I thank God for the strength
I thank God in the end

I give him all the praise
I thank God for my ex

I thank God for my mother
They both could be a real a bitch

I pray the Lord forgives me for calling my mom a bitch
I pray that my ex stops doing bitch shit

I pray for my family my friend my community
I pray for my sister especially

God loves us and he give us the free will to do whatever we want
He tells us to do right and sometime we don't

I know I don't
Not all the time

I pray

Lord forgive me for my sins
Love me even when I don't pray

I know people who won't waste their breath
On someone 'cause they feel like they're not listening

I pray to God God don't feel that way
I pray he hears my prayers I don't say

I pray all the time
I pray for love
And for this I pray

Happy

You can't see her tears
So therefore...

she's happy

as appeared with a smile so sweet from
what your eyes can see...

she's happy

But you don't see her tears
As she passes you by she may wink
May approach you to speak

Just a little conversation
Just to distract the depression
Just to make you think

Damn ain't she's filled with such joy

ain't she happy

But just the night before
She was left all alone
With a house full of people

But no one home
Of course, she's happy
Look at her

She's beautiful
Her walk her talk
She has so much potential

She's got to be happy

Not a friend too overrated
Not a love un-ever lasting
Not a piece of heart gone

So that leaves her to seem happy
                    Just until
You catch those falling tears

Scared of Love

I'm not scared
of lions and tigers or bears

But I'm scared
of loving so much that it hurts

I told him I loved him
but I was afraid

Seems these fears
were relevant 'cause I lived through
my worst nightmare

Guess I should have stuck to my guns

We were just having fun
It was all just a game

But I believed the promises that were made
That our relationship wouldn't change

We were always going to be friends
Used our pinkies for this promise
But I guess it was all elementary

Me exposing my heart

That making a monster out of him
What's worse than a monster? 'cause that's what he'd be

A man pretending to be a friend only to get what he
wants then leaves

But I be Belle and the beast
I slay
Put on my cape and save myself

I Love My Name

Sha Sha gave me the name Shaquan
Not my mom and dad
She had no idea oh the thanksgiving
When deciding to give me the name

Thank you

She just wanted my name to fit in with the rest of the family
Though it is spelled the wrong way it sounds about right
Shaquan (Shu-kran) means

Thank you

in Arabic
Did you know every time you say my name correctly
You would be

Thanking me

I didn't alway like my name
Well I didn't alwats know what it means
People would tease me
Call me Chaka Khan
But I loved her
So that didn't bother me
Some people would shorten it add an i e
Take away the Sha
Call me Quannie
I still love it still means

Thank you

to me
My name rings bells
Set the alarm off in this mutha fucka
Fuck some shit up if it have to

Thank you very much

My name will bring peace unity and hope
To the community

Thank you Jah

Let the voices of our ancestors sing
Shaquan you are born
You light is a gift from above
Wear these gifts with honor and respect
Your name was no accident

Thank you Shaquan

Never forget

Remember

(2)
The butterflies
The heart that melts
I remember love

(3)
How fucked up it was
How it used to use and abuse
Had me confused

(1)
I remember love
How nice it was
I remember how it felt

(4)
Started to be like fuck it
Well fuck you too love
I remember love

(5)
Everything about it
From the beginning
To where I thought it would end...me

(6)
I remember love
The ugly truth and
The beautiful lie

(7)
I remember begging for forgiveness
Like why me love
I love hard and

(8)
I fall even harder
I thought love would've lift me high
Thought we could be this fairy tale

Love

(10)
Had me wondering what did I do to
deserve this love
Was it ever love
What is this roller coaster proclivity

(9)
Who knew love could be so scary
It's hard to look at love
The shit you put me through love

(11)
I don't know what to expect of love
From what it was
Love got me losing all my senses

(12)
Lost in love
Can't control my thought of love
I thought love would kill me

(13)
Love has only made me stronger
But I'm weak for love
Crazy how I still love

(14)
When I remember love
All the things that love put me through
I still manage to love

(15)
Pray for peace to be steel
'Cause damn love

(16)
I remember
I remember love
Remember Love

Gracious Love

She loves unconditionally
        Gives generously
                Expecting nothing in return

Her heart is full
        It holds so much pain
                Endures so much sorrow
                        Yet she is still so joyful

So forgiving
        Shining light in dark places
                Breaking chains

Disrupting the plan of destruction placed before her
                Smiling like she not fighting demons

Like the monsters under her bed don't scream
                Give up you can't win
                        She's winning

The fact that she opened her eyes
                To face another day
                      The battle has already been won

Love Water

Drink me, slurp me up like kool aid. LEt me be all over your tongue, Say my name, Say you need me

, Glisten, make me write the truth, Do I love you, Love on me

Rain for love. Disrupt the drought, Gorw in love, Reflect on me like the sun

I love you, Would you walk on me like Jesus? Or swim and breathe me like a fish. I wish it would

When you thirst, quench me. Love how I love. Give life, Drown you with the way

winters night, your favorite tea. On any given day, I am good. Just enough alone,.

On a summers day, add lemon and sugar. On a cold

Love like water. Like I want to pour into you. Love be like water.

I Am Love

I AM LOVED
I am blessed and highly favored
I am protected

I AM LOVE
I cry my heart out
That does not make me weak

I PRAY
I ask for forgiveness
I do sin but I am not a bad person

I AM LOVED
I am surrounded by people who love me
Who will protect me if someone tries to hurt me

I'VE BEEN HURT
I have asked my protectors to forgive the ones that have hurt me
That is love

I AM WHO I AM

Costing Love

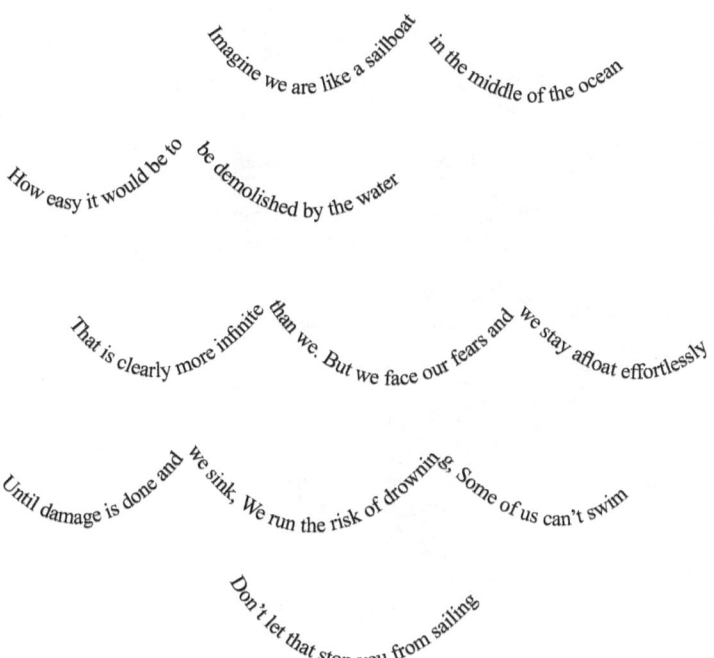

Imagine we are like a sailboat in the middle of the ocean

How easy it would be to be demolished by the water

That is clearly more infinite than we. But we face our fears and we stay afloat effortlessly

Until damage is done and we sink; We run the risk of drowning; Some of us can't swim

Don't let that stop you from sailing

So in Love

If I wrote a love poem to him every morning
I wonder would he think I'm crazy?

Or would he too fall in love?

All I do is think of ways to love him better
Trying to ignore the fact that we fit

That we were made for each other
True love does exist

He's it

I love him

How should I let him know
In a thousand love poems?

Jealous Skies

As sure as
the sun will always rise
on the east and set on the west
I will always love you.... The stars are jealous
of the way I gaze into your eyes

At the way
I find light in them too
How I wanna be where you are
Wherever you are...No matter how far
No matter how hot or how cold the weather
may be

With
all the stars
around me...It's you I'm wishing upon
It's you I long for...You I look to like I do the
sun the moon and the stars....For guidance
for love....My sky

The Photographer and the Poet

Capture the beauty of the world
Write about it
Our story already written
Made in God's plan
Gives me the energy to love
Brings me back to life

He gave me the kind of love that
made me wanna wake up
and make pancakes for him
every morning

Burning Love

Just like the fire was meant to burn
Turn substance back to dust....I was meant to love you
My love be like a diamond in the rough...made to sustain the
heat and the pressure... What would become of it
Would be worth more than diamonds
Worth more than life
itself

Action

If
my love
story was a
movie and I was
the director of it…
I would make it so
that we would never end.
There would be a happily ever after. Fireworks would erupt and when the credits
roll our names would appear in bold…My love and I Followed by pictures
and bloopers of us laughing. However the game goes we would
both win. A solid tie, Not an eye for an eye. Instead, we would
stay in love. We wouldn't lose each other this time. We'd
move on to the next chapter have a dozen sequels.
Three or four remakes. And we would be one.
We would never end. The love would
never Stop. We'd start over and over
again. Fall deeper and stronger in love
every time. In this love story there's a
door the door is always open. Love is
always welcomed.   It can come and
go as it please.   But in my story
it never   leaves

Dopamine

High off love…Love had me higher than expected. Higher than I ever been
Now how do I get down from here? The way that I loved him you would
think ..No else wanted me…I thought he really loved me
Thought he was the one. Silly me…Who said to get
that high? I knew I should have kept my
feet firmly on the ground I should
have known he didn't really
love me.Now look at me
Knocked off cloud
Nine.I know what
I gotta do. Suck
it up, wipe the
tears away
It's a cold
game out
here.
Hearts
will be
broken
Protect yours

My Man Be Like This

I'm wondering if my man is ecstasy
'Cause I'm telling you man he gets to me
I mean I'm so high

I'm touching the sky forget the butterflies
I'm mesmerized MAGNIFIED

I mean I'm stuck
Love struck

And I don't want to get a w a y
I'm hoping we stay together forever no matter the situation

he's introduced me to the LIGHTS of love
that I never knew could shine so brightly
is it the way that he touches me that's got me tripping
'Cause I'm telling you I'm going HYPHY

He like my dope
Got me feenin for more

Showers me with *kisses*
And I'm never his mistress

I'm more like wifey and he's my fellow sidekick
Like BONNIE AND CLYDE

We in it till we die
If only you knew what this real love could do to you

I've found my soulmate

And please don't hate 'cause that means when your
man is trying to get with me

I won't give him no play anyway
'Cause that's right I love my boo

And if you had him you'd love him too
If you try to take what's mine best believe
It'd be suicide but never mind that

Let's get back to the facts on where I was at

How my man treats me so good

And loves me like no one else could
And I can talk to him like he's my **best friend**

And call on him when I need somebody to depend on
He's my ENERGY

My wind beneath my wings
I love him so

And I will never let him go
He holds the key to my heart

And there's a wire attached to his that makes it spark
He may not be the smartest person in the world

But he's the *poetic* spirit I do adore and he's mine
May not always there when I call but he's always on time

And I'll give him my all in the drop of a dime
Even in my highest points of tipsiness
I promise to never tell his secrets
For the thought of the vibe of him leaves me speechless

Which has got me thinking
Is my man ecstasy

'cause I'm telling you man he gets to me
I mean I'm so high

I'm touching the sky forget the *butterflies*
I'm mesmerized **MAGNIFIED**
I mean I'm stuck
Love has ~~struck~~

Lay Down Your Love

Clear your head from the past

Instead let the spirit of joy manifest

Rejoice at all times
Even when you've been betrayed
Even when your heart's been broken into pieces

Grit the heavy

Lay down your burden

Give it to God

Giggle

Smile like your heart still believes it is loved

Girl

Girl
Young girl

Girl who cries
Girl who seems forgettable

When you gonna grow up girl
You ain't woman yet

Still girl
Convince yourself you are beautiful again

A delicate flower cutting all who touch
you the
wrong way

Young girl
Silly girl

 Girl who still believes in miracles
That still believes somewhere the sun still
shines

Hopeful you are
Change the world you are
Leave it in the hands of the young

A girl with power
A girl who still dreams
be that girl
You are such a fucking beast

Building Love

Currently under construction
love is home. I'd like to say I
live there comfortably. Trying
not to disturb anyone. Trying
not to wake the ones who may be
sleeping, I'm walking silently. Trying to keep the
peace. But this house of love is so messy.   I trip.
So unorganized not sure where anything goes I
think it's about time for some spring cleaning. Yeah
it's time to do some redecorating. Tear down some of these walls.
Make room for something new I have a lot baggage. I've put it in
the closet.   A lot of things need to goI think it's about time I air
out this dirty laundry. It's long overdue Inside this house I've made
a home, Full of potential, Currently under construction.

He said he will never talk to me again
I said say word
I said I love you
He said nothing
I heard him

This Is Love Too

The devil ain't got shit on my mother
I bet he calls her for tips on how to fuck up somebody's day
My daddy ain't got time for the bullshit
I figured he'd come around to rescue me
when he remembers he said he was coming
He is not the elephant in the room
But I decorate his picture
even when he's not around
He gets me
He'll be here
once he's done with everyone else first
Love is two-faced
But I still want to be married
I mean just because love slapped me in the face
doesn't mean love doesn't love me
My momma did and my momma love me
And it's okay that love broke its promise 'cause
So did my dad and I know he loves me
Momma and Daddy love me
As dysfunctional as that love may be
It's still love to me

I Am Human

This is me being human
Or at least as human as I can be

I'm not of this world
At least I don't want to be

And this is human
Crying at times

Having this unsustainable sense of emotions
Having to heal from the trauma

Endure it then release it
Then endure it again

And this is human to me
We are human being nothing less than great

I am a good human
At least I try to be

Feels like I'm not of this world even when I'm trying to be
But I can't be you man I can only be me

I am happy
I am all smiles

Even when I'm hurting
I am a celebration

A twinkle in the eye
I am beautiful

Even on my worst days
I am love

I am so much love
I am so giving of all this love

And I don't regret it
I don't take it back

And this is human of me
Only this isn't human of me

This is the God in me
But I am human today

Fuck You With a Smile

FUCK YOU
to the hypocritical Christians that judged me before even getting to know me because
of how I dressed
No I wasn't trying to take your man
No I wasn't trying to get your attention
I was just simply being comfortable in my own skin

FUCK YOU
for making me feel that i shouldn't be

FUCK YOU
to all my exes
To go over every single individual
FUCK
would take entirely too long so lets
Simplify by saying
FUCK YOU
to the one that cheated that should narrow it down to all except for one who deserves
his very own special
FUCK YOU
for doing everything else but

FUCK YOU
to the bitches that tried to sabatage my name
You only got them looking closer at me now they watching how I shine

Yeah
FUCK YOU BITCH
Now you bitch but to the bitch that got a problem with me getting this off of my chest

FUCK YOU
insecurity

FUCK YOU
doubt

FUCK YOU
depression

I want to
FUCK YOU UP
right now

As a matter of fact
FUCK
my bitch ass neighbor
MUTHA FUCKA
called parking enforcement on me three

MUTHA FUCKING
times!

If I get another
MUTHA FUCKING
ticket I'm
FUCKING
your ass up and
FUCK
yo green ass grass that
MUTHA FUCKAS
gone be brown and yellow now how bout that
FUCK
that bitch too

FUCK
Donald Trump

FUCKITY FUCK FUCK
running out of
FUCKS
to give

Nothing
FUCKING
matters

You see we gotta remind you black lives do
FUCK
you all live

FUCK
who you want to
FUCK
and
FUCK
you to the ones that
FUCK
the ones that don't want to be
FUCKED
you
FUCKING
rapist you
almost made me loose my smile and
FUCK
you for that
I giving a lot of
FUCKS FUCKING
smiling 'cause I don't give a
FUCK

FUCK YOU, with a smile

57

Offerings

My offering
If you want to
Take this love why don't you
Take my hands hold them
Wrap your arms around me and hold me
Promise me you'll never leave me
That you will always protect me
That I am always loved
With no conditions …
No?
Only when you feel like it
No?
Only after you get over it
After your temper tantrum
After the damage has already been done?
Who's gonna protect me from you huh?
Be my love why don't you
The love I've always wanted
I know we can't be who we want us to be
I still want love to love me
I promise I will always love
Even when it cuts deep
Still love while healing the wounds
I'll try to hold no record of wrong
Forgive me if I pick at the scabs from the scars
I want to forget
I'm still healing

I find something beautiful in writing through the pain

Its love

I Love My Mother

I love her

And I only say it because I have to

They told me to
They say she's the only one that I got so I oughta
She gave me life so I betta

Forgive everything that she's done
"She's your mother"

I love her

She is beautiful

Try to tell her she is not
And that would be hating
And she will fuck you up

Put some respect on her name
That bitch will show you who a real one is

She is the realest
Mommie dearest

Don't make her have to remind you
Don't you dare do to her what she do to you
You know like keep it real speak your heart

Be unapologetic about it
She will fuck you up

Who do you think you are she is the HBIC
and don't you forget it

Don't you ever think you too old to get fucked with
She will fuck with you but you betta be pretty
She don't fuck with no bum bitches
Old bum bitch

I love her

She told me she love me too
She really do

She's also told me
I don't want you

Ain't nobody ever gonna want you
And I love you but I don't like you

And I believe it
I feel the same way

Gotta love her

I hate her sometimes

Sometimes I wish she never had me
She does too
She told me so

She doesn't remember saying this but
I will never forget
It's ok I forgive her

I love her

Not only because I have to
Swear I wouldn't fuck with her if I didn't have to
If the people she swear turned me against her didn't tell me to

"That's your mother" they said
"You only got one" they said

She's only trying to make you stronger for this world
Is what I convinced myself that she's doing
'Cause no one has hurt me more than she has

And no one ever will
I love her for that

I love how she just don't give a fuck
I hate how she just don't give a fuck

She could be the sweetest thing in the world
But she could be the meanest thing in the world
If you make her that way
Don't take much to make her that way
a thin line between love and hate

My mother has taught me patience
My mother has taught me respect
Everything that I know

How love could be so unloving at times
You can still call it love
if you have to

I Am My Mother's Child

I never wanted to be like her

My mother
Her fire fury

I used to say the devil ain't got shit on my momma

I've seen her shoot
And she don't aim to kill

She like to watch a muthafucka suffer

Watch them bleed
Give them a band-aid
Then snatch it off
Just evil

Can't help but be mean
Call it being real

It is never necessary

I wonder sometimes what it would be like
if I didn't forgive her
Would you forgive someone who left you in the streets
After they forgot about you

Told you that you weren't shit to them anymore
when I was a little girl
At times I felt like no one's daughter

Malikia told me to forgive her
Said that she was the only one that I got
That she loved me even though she said some fucked up shit

Said I was no longer her daughter
She didn't mean it

She doesn't mean what she say
She was always going to be my mother

She didn't have a choice
We didn't have a choice

She loves me

A Letter To My Unborn Child

If they ask you why I never had children
You tell them it's because I never wanted them
You tell them that this world is so cruel and complex
That I don't even want to be in it
So why would I subject you to this bullshit
World so hectic yet I embrace it with a smile
with such grace

Would be the epitome of what a
good mother should be
But see that's just it

You would change all that
For you I'd say fuck the world
Though I already do that with a smile now
For you I'd be a little more aggressive with it
Screaming and determined that you can't have my child
You won't know pain like me
Get neglected like me
feel like me

Not wanting to be here
And if you did I would kill you
How dare you not appreciate all I would do for you
I would live for you

I've already wanted to die
But this world needs my smile
It needs just a little bit of created happiness
But if you were here my world would revolve around you
The man I created you with would be jealous of you
'Cause I probably loved him more than anything in
this world up until you arrived but fuck him too
I would make you the exception

And the only exception to why life is worth living
For without you here
It would be ok to die
You were better off dead than alive
You're welcome

Surviving Love

Love and I
We go way back
Got history

I figured if my love was more like a 90s R&B love song
then maybe it would have survived
how did I survive

I don't know
I thought I died
I thought I'd be dead by now

This is not the first time
I've tried takin my life into my own hand
Giving it away

As if it is mines to give
I live for love
Yet it is love that kills me

Fortunately I am held in the hand of a high power that loves me
like no other
I know this 'cause the pills were too hard to swallow and the
trigger wouldn't pull

I look to others who rest peacefully and wonder why not me
when I've been begging to come home since the beginning
My purpose has yet to be redeemed

So much work to do and I don't even know what I'm doing
So I cry
I let these marinate until I find the strength to wipe them away

I always find the strength I am still searching for my way
Thriving with every step for I am favored
and I don't know how
but I survive

Why Now

Why now I've cried all the tears that I could cry
I'm done wishing I would die
And I accepted the fact that you didn't love me
as much as you should

Don't get it twisted I'm glad you finally came to your
senses and acknowledge the wishes I made when I was six
years old however many years later but why now
I'm finally getting over the fact that you're not here

The phase of running to other men trying to fill that
love that isn't there and I'm through looking in the
mirror and crying 'cause I look just like you and
besides your name birthday

I know nothing about you
So why now
Why come into my life
After all this time and be something you should
have been from the get go

Why now after I've forgotten all the things I wanted to
say and faced the fact that I am what I am
Conceived by a man that just don't give a damn
I don't have enough fingers enough toes enough
strands of hair

To count the many times you've lied to me so
Why not now
Why not start all over
Hi my name is Shaquan and I am your daughter

My Ghetto Version of Shakespeare

To be or not to be

That is my question
In love with a man that claims to be the sweetest
thing and you'll vouch right along for him for you
see it in his eye but is it right to be or not to be
'Cause he love another
But there's a connection of affection
but he kisses and touches on all the right places
so to be or not to be
in love with him would be crazy
So should I be or not be
In love with the man I dream of at night as I
hold my pillow tight wondering if he feels the same way as I
To be oh I've got to be
'Cause there is no one else I've thought of like this
And oh how I wish I could be in his arms at this very moment
Look into his eyes and tell him how much I want him
that if he be toast then I be starving
to be or not to be
somebody please tell me

When Trees Fall

If a Tree Falls in the
Forest and No One's Around, Would It Make a Sound?
Would you hear it. With all the tragedy going on in the world.
If you were standing right in front of it you probably wouldn't even
see it so busy with your eyes opened wide shut and ears focused on
unimportant stuff. That the one thing that means the most to you is a
goddamn cell phone. Yet there is a child somewhere that can't find its way
home and that doesn't even have a home to find and yet you're sitting here
mad wondering why so-n-so hasn't called. Got you rolling eyes at the same person
that greets you with a smile and makes sure you're alright before you leave in
the morning but that same nigga who called you a bitch and try to make up
for it with a kiss you forgave him for it then deceive me when all I'm
trying to do is keep your head in focus. And it's making me sick to
my stomach   'cause you can't   see that it's
hurting everyone
around you. I
keep telling
you they're
trying to kill
our dreams
but you thinking
I'm looking
down on you.
But that ain't the
issue. Every night
I get down on my
knees and I pray for
you hoping that one day you
open your eyes and see the path
that God has laid for you ,'Cause when the tears of our fears fall you don't seem to
hear the real meaning of the words I love you and that scares me. 'Cause your trees
are falling while you're gone doing what you are doing and it's screaming devoting
cursing but where are you even when you are not around it's calling to you
whether you hear it or not

Not a Love Song

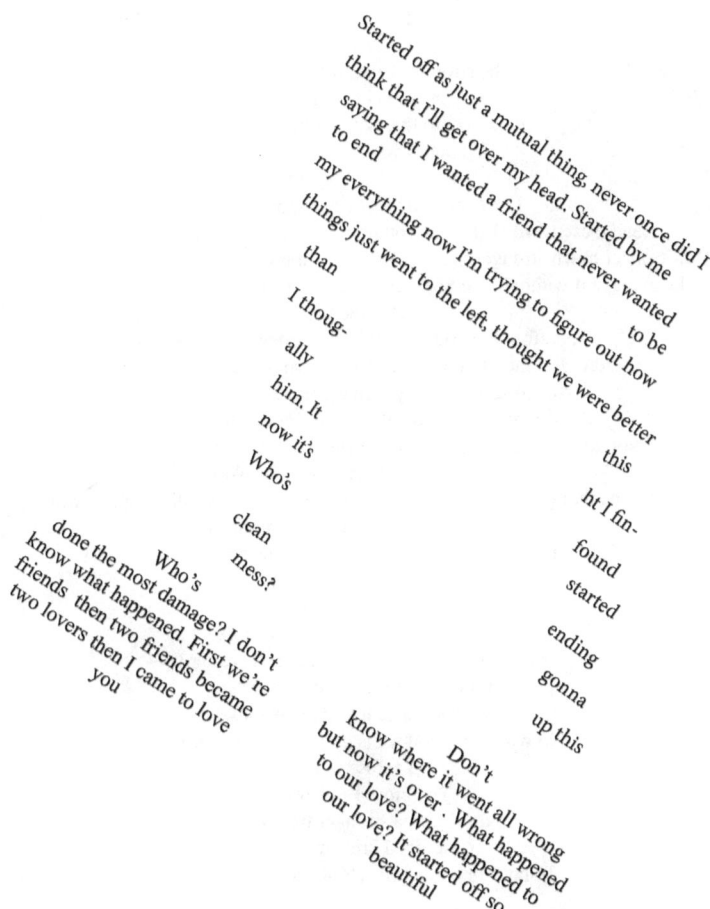

Started off as just a mutual thing, never once did I think that I'll get over my head. Started by me saying that I wanted a friend that never wanted to end to be my everything now I'm trying to figure out how things just went to the left, thought we were better than this I thoug- ht I fin- ally found him. It started now it's ending Who's gonna up this clean mess?

Who's done the most damage? I don't know what happened. First we're friends then two friends became two lovers then I came to love you

Don't know where it went all wrong but now it's over . What happened to our love? What happened to our love? It started off so beautiful

69

Stronger

Last night I cried wondering how I could live without him
Couldn't see myself being without him
But I gotta hold on be strong learn how to get along with this shit 'cause
It seems I have to live with it
And I could live without his tender kiss
Though I wish we never did it
Though I don't want to lose
I'm gonna do what I'm supposed to do
Read these words I'll show you how I could make it without that love
I'm stronger much stronger than yesterday for it didn't kill me as far as I can see it
I can make it without love no words of goodbye are gonna tear down my life
Refusing to cry
Therefore I am much stronger, stronger than yesterday
It didn't kill me as far as I can see it I can make it without his love
No words of goodbye are gonna tear down my life
I'm refusing to cry therefore I'm much stronger
Not that tears are a sign of weakness I've just cried enough already
I told myself I was gonna be okay
But the thought of him confuses me I didn't think it would end this way
Why is this love thing so complicated
It's like he led on then kept it going until he sent me on my way
Yes it hurt so much
Broke my heart to the core
But I can't dwell on it any more
I'm stronger so much stronger than yesterday
It didn't kill me as far as I can see
I could make it without his love
No words of goodbye is gonna tear down my life
I refuse to cry
Therefore I'm stronger
So much more stronger than yesterday
Yesterday I cried my eyes out
Today I'm telling myself it's going to be alright

Danzel

I didn't want to love him
I didn't want him at first
He came to rescue me
Saved me when I should have been saving myself
I'm mad 'cause I felt safe in his arms

And I wasn't

I prayed him out and still it was hard to let go
I still hold him deep in my heart
Even though he betrayed my trust
Put a gun to my face
Told me he'd shoot it

Triggered

I barely dodged the bullet
Grazed in the back of my spine
I let him get away with murder
But I rose from the dead
As delicate as concrete made me
scuffed and gritted and blood red
Heart still full of love for a man who loves me no more

Or never did

I Care

Just care

A little be a lot
The minimum of pay paid
But it ain't about the money
I care
I break my back it's so heavy
Get slapped spit on
Still giving all this love
This care
Smile in place
I'm mad I'm here
I could be striving towards my dreams
bearing these bills like lights
Like gas … like gas
Like ... don't let my car break down
How I'm gonna get there
But here I am
I'm here caring
And they don't care though
They forget my name
They remember I care though
Show up
When blood should be thicker
Still caring
While you lying to me
Telling me that it is when it isn't
Still caring
Chained by foot on an invisible hook
I care but it's just for decoration
'Cause I can leave at any time but
Here I am
caring
I still care

The Breakup

He didn't come up to   me and say let's talk
Instead he started acting   funny
Started canceling   plans at the last minute
He didn't say   no it's not you it's me
He said   I'm tripping
Like I came up with this   illusion that he was being distant
I said I love you   and he didn't say it back
Like what you don't   love me anymore
He said I   never did
At first I   thought he was joking
But he   meant it
Love   ended before I noticed
The breakup was   happening and
I was holding   on to something that was
never   there
Like   I imagined it
He played   fiddle
I   heard the music
He claimed   to have deaf ears
Labeled me   fool said how could I ever love you
You are   you
But I thought he   did

I Love Hard

I love you like it's easy
Bend and break for you
Do all the things you want me to
And you don't even love me
You take happily
As I give more and more each day
And I remain loyal
While you go and look for someone else to love you like me
Ask me to remain humble
So I don't fuck shit up
Like I ought to
So I fuck shit up
Like I ought to
But not as bad as I wanted to it's not like I busted the windows out your car
Ok so I tried to but I missed
Thank God I didn't backtrack and go bad back to my old ways
When I did what I meant and I meant what I said
Like when I said I would kill you and I would have got convicted
I wish you were devoted to me
As much as I was to
the thought of us
A fairy tale of love
Instead this nightmare
from the one I used to dream of
I have to endure this
Still no matter what
I love you
I love hard
I love you like it's easy
It's not

Love Rain

Love
rain down on
me and fill me up
till my cup overflow
and give it to those who
are not worthy. I still love 'em.
Even when the slit of my tongue
throws daggers. With words that cut
deep. Saying things they don't mean like.
Stupid bitch

Still love, Come rain, Come storm love me. Oh don't
you love … love that feeling of love. When you don't
want to but you still do. Ok so I hate that but, I still love it
too. Don't you hate it when you tell yourself to stop, Loving
them but you can't. It be love, Let it take control, Let it pour
down like rain, Heavy. Never too much. However much is
needed love bigger than all the seas. Let it grow taller than
the highest trees. And when the rain's done...

Let not the love end
Even through the rain the sun is shining somewhere
Let love reign in the darkest hour
I love him like there's no tomorrow
I'll spend forever in today
Even if it rains

This Could be our Love Song

I want to touch fuck feel you, Want you to arc de triomphe. Hold me close,

don't let me go, I'm bout to come over. I would really like to take it all the

way. Feel you deep inside, let me ride you, switch, pause, don't stop. This

could be our love song. Come make love to me. You can say I need you, I just

want to please you. Then switch, pause, don't stop. Now pardon my french but

Voulez-vous coucher avec moi, ce soir. Now I don't want to be rude but I want

you, Right here, right now, we can we start off slow then go faster and deeper

Starting something that can last forever, I just want you to know that I want

you the most. More than anybody that I ever wanted before. I would really

like to take it all the way. Feel you deep inside me, let me ride you then switch

pause, don't stop. This could be our love song, now come make love to me.

You can say I need you, But I just want to please you, then switch pause don't stop.

God of Forgiveness

This don't mean you can come back in and let me down again come and break my heart more than want you already did. Maybe just love me, rub my body after you take the knife out of my back. I'll unswallow the bitch I called you for leaving me haging when I needed you the most. Queen of forgiveness God even You don't have acces to my hurt no more Call if you want, I'll answer

My First Love

We met and my heart didn't skip a beat
My mother had just told me I wasn't her daughter anymore
At the time I was just a virgin
But now on the hunt for someone to de-flower
Me I was hurting and I wanted the hurt to feel good
He asked me if I was going to homecoming
I didn't know where to go for home
I just wanted to be numb
All I wanted to do was fuck get drunk
Find someone to roll up my blunt
I didn't know how to roll myself at the time
I got more than what I asked for
I didn't want a child
I was still a child
I thought I was having fun
Abort mission return to sender
And my PE teacher told me to keep running
I was too weak I fell down
He came out of nowhere to pick me up
And I thought
Oh this is love I have found
Carried me to safety
You rescued me and I didn't have to ask
Had gun to my temple
And he called to say hey
I was just thinking of dying
I didn't think anyone was thinking of me
But then he called
he saved me from that bullet that day
My own trigger-happy therapy
And I dedicated my life to loving him always
He saved me
And he didn't even know it
Broken hearts and promises would later kill me
But he was my captain save a hoe
I had some demons I needed to get under control
But I knew I loved him
Only had to let go of him because he didn't love me back
That didn't stop the love though
It would only grow and grow
Into love overflow
Even though I don't show it as much as used to
I still do love him
Always will

My Everything

He's my everything
All my thoughts and dreams
He lights my fire I'm in flames
In a sourceless power got me in a daze
And he takes me higher than outer space
'Cause he knows where we going
And strives me to get there
he's more than my lover
Nothing could compare
That's my baby
What a precious creator
I can't let demons destroy this perfect picture
Don't you lose the one you love for the one that you lust
'cause it would be terrible
To let go of true love

Love Number Too

When he met me I thought I was Trina
Mista minna
That pull over 'cause I was too too pretty
My confidence was on level 10
I knew I was going to be something
I was just waiting for someone to discover me
He discovered I was naive
Only 17 but I thought I was grown
At first I didn't want him
Then my momma left me in the middle of the road
I was tryna call someone else on the phone
My daddy gone and my granny gone
Both out of town
They would have come to get me hands down
I was scrolling through my phone
I wasn't gonna call him
He didn't even have a car
I had niggas who had Lexus trucks and Bens
He was not the one I was checking
but he called me
I told him my story and he came and got me and that was it
Now I was devoted
He made me promise to tell my first love I had a new love

And I did but he didn't really love me either

Shots Fired

I give this heart of mine. Unshielded with anticipation that this love be reciprocated
And when it's not I proceed to do the most.My intention being to
do to others as I would want done to me. The hunter peeps this
thus preys upon this blessing. Call the sacrifice a holy service.
The blood shed shot from the gun and I pulled the trigger. Determined to be loved

Keep On Turning

We made music together so I thought
We was gonna be the next Ike and Tina

We *were* the next Ike and Tina

Only I hit him back the first time he hit me
We were fighting while rolling down the river
I was high off shit I didn't even know it was
Had me all the way fucked up

Stuck on stupid

I called it a fatal attraction
That's actually what he called me

If looks could kill
I would have dead it before entering the relationship

Skipped the bullet wisping past my ribs
Broken glass and busted windows

The watered down mics and beat box kit
Stomped on Gucci glasses

You can't see me
I'm hiding behind the smile

Dickmatized and calling it love
All 'cause he came to my rescue

And now I must run

It would be ungodly of me
to not be honest
and call a spade a spade
a stupid hoe
a stupid hoe
and
love love

She's Having Your Baby

It took everything that I had inside not to die that day

But I died that day

Laid in bed and could not move for three days
Couldn't breathe for weeks
Those words damn near killed me

She's having your baby

She told me

And I tried to say I was fine
I was going to be ok

Heart choked up on
You and her and she knew how I felt
The love I had for you
She was my friend
Play cousin
You were my best friend
My whole world

The one that I run to
And she's having your baby
The baby I didn't want to conceive
Don't baby momma me
I wanted to spend my life with you without the complications

But she's having your baby

Had your baby

Said she's sorry she hurt me
Knew this would hurt me

Choosing life over my heart
A heartbeat
Heart beat loud
I don't want to hear it see it
I missed the first steps

I missed the first steps

                    Denial

                              I heard she was having your baby

                    I loved her
                              I loved you
                    Not together

Wiped tears from being torn up on what we are now
I guess she wanted to know what that pain felt like
                    to be loved by you too

                              Only she's having your baby
                                  Something I wouldn't do

                    Baby

I close my eyes and I delete everybody attached
that could pull up the image of this child
I would rather pretend this doesn't exist

                              My momma said y'all not my friend
                              He don't love you she don't love you
                    And this time I put up no argument

How I'm gonna compete with a baby

                              Now lay me down to sleep and wake me when
                                  Better yet don't wake me
                                  She's having your baby
                                          boy
                    You gotta be kidding me

Hardest pill to swallow
was realizing that I didn't mean

- anything -

to people that meant

EVERYTHING

to me

That New York Love

Yo dead ass I don't want no dead ass friends

Fuck a fake friend

Be a friend
Fuck a friend

Be like family
Fuck the family

Be like Jesus
Now what would Jesus do

Be like fuck em
Ignore those calls

Dead ass
I don't want no dead as friends

Unless they gonna forgive me like Jesus
I don't want no half ass friends

What I can't get mad
Nigga I'm human

Oh your love comes with conditions
Can I not do no wrong

Do I gotta do everything you say
Nah son

I don't want it
I don't need that kind of pressure
Nigga you ain't no diamond maker

Yo dead ass I don't no dead ass friends

That's All I Got

I promise I will not abandon my best friend
I gotta be my own best friend now
My best friend abandoned me
Mad at me
Left me for dead
What did i do
Love you and talk shit
Speak my mind
Gave you too much of this heart
Was I too much spice from the sweet side you got used to
Don't matter now
I'm living for me
My best friend that's all I got
Everything I do I do it out of love
You ain't gotta love me
I love myself
I promise I will hold my hand when I'm scared
I won't judge me for my mental breakdown
Or call me weird or weak
For expressing my feelings
I'll encourage it
I live for it
Shout out to the best friends that didn't disappear when shit got tough
When shit got real
Who was there for me when I needed it most

Me
From now on I'm my own best friend

I want to feel love

I want to get off

Like really put an orgasm into a poem

I want to write from a healed point of view

A happy place

Ma Lik

He said I taste like something he has never had before
And he wants to taste it forever
He said he gotta have it, it gotta be mine
Giddy drips from my nectarine got his taste bud thriving, juices flowing
Slurp me up eat me out
Fuck me till i can't cum no more
I suck on his finger tips
He kiss me under my navel
Go where he won't go
And he don't stop till I say so
Say my name
Call me Daddy
Gushy waters
Come take a sip of this overflow
Waterfall my clementine
Cherry pick this blossom with your tongue
Write me a love letter
With no hands
Fuck the shit out of me
The vibrations are exquisite
I burst and he indulges in every drop
Calls me candy
Calls me now and later, life saver, gusher
Popped
Quenched
Served pleasure on a platter
Spoons full of this pussy
Dive in
Swim in this ocean
Rock me to sleep
With this pussy in his mouth
I asked what do I taste like
He said like nothing I ever had in this life time
Bet
He ate it the mourning
He gonna eat me again tonight

Love Lens

I had a vision of love
And apparently I was the only one who could see it
Though my love was unconditional
Yours had its limits
How can I say I love you and you don't even like me
How do you want me but not want me
And like a sex fiend
I give myself to you
As if I can't get better
As if I don't deserve more
Is it because I hope you are capable
Do you like to hurt me
There's nothing more painful
Than to love and not be loved enough
My heart bleeds blue
It is weeping
Drowning itself in tears for you
I promised myself not to love so much again
And yet somehow how I always find myself here
Wiping tears
Picking up the pieces blindly trying to put them together again
An image only I could imagine
Could fathom
But if only you could see
How beautiful

Love You

.

There's this love for you like you'll never know

When you want it you can get it

Don't have to take it slow 'cause it's been waiting

Your love has been waiting for you for so long

Why wait any longer?

Love yourself

Why do I have to keep having to remind you that you are
beautiful?

I know your smile is broken
your heart has been torn all up
But don't give up on love
Don't give up on

you

To My Sister

Sister, I love you,

You be on my mind
Sister you are one of a kind
Sister my heart is filled with so much love for you
I know you think I don't know nothing
But Sister I do
And oh sister have I got news for you
I think you're something
I hope you think that you're something too
But did you know you are my everything
Did you know I asked mommie for you
I begged for a sister
I had no idea God would bless me with such a blessing
You're such an angel my best friend
When best friends fell off I had you to hold my hand
Through the rough times you taught me that being tough ain't always about fighting
You taught me that standing tall could be as simple as smiling
As you give me a reason to smile
Do you know that
There are very few good people in the world
I'm happy to say that you are one of them
Did you know that
You give me joy in my darkest days
I wake every day by God's grace and for my sister
Oh sister
If only you knew
How much I love oh how

I love you,

Sister

Give Me Love

It's giving me
Don't take this life for granted
For the light the flowers look on to
I see the same sun
With breath from the same air
An environment surrounded by my worst fears
Calling it courage
Maybe I'm just suicidal
Take this love
Hit it hard
With every brick thrown to the wall
build relationships
knock them down
Start all over again
For love give everything
Till there's no more to give

Rest in Love

Ashes to ashes
      dust to dust

Love be a test to us and sometimes we fall short
Somehow I gotta except that there will never be another us
What was left of us is now ruined
Poeple act like they dont want to fix what's broken
Would rather dispose of it move on from what was and go find something new

That is something we do
      That is an option

But when you value something you cherish right?
Sometimes that cherished moment has to be a memory
Remembering the love will shine again
The sun goes down but the sun always shining

Give it time to show up
      From dawn to dusk from dusk to dawn

How ever you count the hours
It may not be the way you want but there will always be love

God is love
      I am a poet

Sometime I get a littile crazy emotional
Sometimes I can't hold my liquor
I may talk shit
Call you a bitch and tell you I love you in the same sentence
It is the way God has made me
I try not to be like everybody else
Dub me exclusive

I make my own rules
        Sometimes I break them

              I am the creator of this story
              God sets the destination

              But ultumitly I get to choose
              Put the ashes that turn to dust
              On a path I set for us

I may take a detour
        It is an option

              Wise enough to know what is not in my control
              One being how you feel
              I spoke life into ashes
              And corrupted the soil in which this love was built
              Couldn't make you love me

              Inhaled you
              you took my breath away
              somehow
              I still live

              I let my tear fall
              created an ocean
              Rivers made it to the amazon

For us I cry

              They say only you can prevent forest fires
              And thats not true sometimes you can't help it
              Sometimes destruction happens naturally
              Somethings were not built to last forever

Jaded

Even
out of sight you are always
on my mind. When did I lose my
power? And why did I give it to you?
When you have the ability to hurt me?
Cut me open and turn me out? And I let
you. Gave you the bullet and the gun. Said
"hit me" I'd bite it. I knew you would shoot.
You got good aim. Got it right on the target.
My heart, I die, I rise again. Then I give you
gasoline and matches, you strike it. Watch
me burn. I rise again another resurrection.
This time I'm something new. Something
unnoticeable. This time no weapon form-
ed against me shall prosper I'd say. Knife
in hand of my best friend, Finds my back,
Kills me another beautiful death. Covered
in lies and flaws. Dressed all pretty, Makes
it sound more flattering.That I can't hide
the fact that I can't get you out of my mind.

I Love Love

I LOVE to love

I've been loving as long as I can remember
Been loving even after love don't love me no more

And I love that about me

Love this vulnerable heart of mine
I dissect the pieces fill them up with affirmations of self-love

When I can't find the words myself
I reach out to find those who love and hope for love

Pray my fingertips be equipped to write
Standing on the remembrance of what may not have been love but still remembering
the love that came out of it

I pray I write like concrete set in stone
May be hard to carve out but in due time beautiful and strong

I love how easy it is for me to fall in love
Even though I know it's hard to get back up again

The anticipation of love got me
not wanting to give up on love

Rather I let it go or
hold on to it
its love

Is the love that you have the love you desire?